The Met Office Advises Caution

Rebecca Watts was born in Suffolk in 1983 and currently lives in Cambridge. In 2014 she was one of the Poetry Trust's Aldeburgh Eight, and in 2015 a selection of her work was included in Carcanet's *New Poetries VI* anthology. *The Met Office Advises Caution* is her first collection.

The Met Office
Advises Caution

REBECCA WATTS

To Violet,
with best wishes.
from RWatts - 7.2.2019.

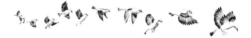

CARCANET

First published in Great Britain in 2016 by

Carcanet Press Limited
Alliance House, 30 Cross Street
Manchester M2 7AQ
www.carcanet.co.uk

A CIP catalogue record for this book is available from
the British Library, ISBN 9781784102722

The publisher acknowledges financial assistance
from Arts Council England.

Contents

THE MET OFFICE ADVISES CAUTION

Realism

Look at the tree.
How it holds out its arms,
waiting for birds to alight.
How it stands on the bank
with or without
company, so sure of its place:
a prop
for the sagging sky,
a relief
from all this flat.

Below the tree
free-riding on the water
a shadow plays,
beguiling,
ripe for idolatry.

I believe the tree
and note it down as the answer
to its own question.

Letter from China

It is not the force of nature
that holds the country in perpetual winter

but the facts of arithmetic
and a fear of winter.

Ask the elderly,
they know what life costs:

once forced to sow seeds,
eyes fixed on the future,

they saw themselves wading
into old age

and reckoned
that a son could keep them afloat

but a daughter is like
spilled water.

So it was
that those who reached the light were dealt with

quickly
in a bucket beside the bed,

while those whom fortune allowed to be glimpsed
curled in the dark womb

were dislodged, dug out, disposed of
before they could begin to flower;

to make way for boys
with strong shoulders.

This was the calculation.
That was their hope.

Now we live in a lopsided sum,
looking onto a wilderness

where scores of unsettled men
conspire:

bare branches
pricking the landscape.

Hopeless together
they clamour for fire.

Saturday Morning, Gorilla Kingdom

You wear your hands like gloves, a slick of black
that's sometimes purple, depending on the angle.

I watch; you separate a grain of matter from the woodchip floor
to chew over. I'd love to see you busy with a Rubik's Cube,

clacking and twisting like no one was looking: fingers
giving your eyes a run for their money, and the game away readily.

Such hands, it's said, could take a typewriter to infinity and bring back
Shakespeare. I wouldn't say that, standing here. We could

shake on something, but you probably wouldn't want to.
Waving seems the only thing to do. I offer mine straight up:

paled by cold, stiff. Self-consciousness,
like arthritis, weakens the grip.

Hawk-Eye

                    There
        in the dash

    little flash of
            brown, optimist
                    doing her best
        against the green
            down,
                    running...

Everything is one under the sky for me;
            the wind is a wall
but
        I see straight
through and the knowledge makes me
        brazen against the white

            She might sense
        I'm coming
                – then quicken my
stooping

My feet are golden. They catch me
            anything

Emmeline's Ascent

Back when her kind should've kept
the fact of ankles to themselves,
it was mildly surprising:
that from the ground – where her

neat boots were tied with satin bows
and her knees, unremarked on, stood
fixed beneath a triple skirt and had not
one single scar to boast of – she

thought to ascend the small stepladder
borrowed for the job from someone's father
and, loosely grasping the hand of a stranger,
swing brilliantly from the hip one long

athletic leg over the rim, into unsupported
territory, without even a pale second
given over to the fear of falling the five
shameful feet back to zero, from such

a high wheel; and that once in the saddle
she recognised herself seeing not what
she never before could've imagined,
but everything exactly as it was – the

clear hard road, made for going along;
the terraces lined up for her admiration;
and on the other side of the clipped hedge
the unhatted men in the park,

a few streets from closed offices,
airing their balding crowns
to the pigeons and anyone else geared up
for once to peer down on them from above.

Map

Pinned to the bedside wall, my map
of the British Isles charts temperaments,
anticipates our movements. Its colouring
is arbitrary and without consequence,

except this morning – when, waking too early,
I see that we are both from yellow places
and that while mine spreads out hazily
like an egg frying in a pan

yours is strung up on tenterhooks,
policed by a high-voltage fence,
charged on all sides by blue electrodes.

Then I look at the counties we escape to:

unfolded from the spine of the great north road,
North Yorkshire is a green paint butterfly
freshly opened, poised to be taken in
or to float us up to Northumberland, which spills

into lakes down west, to sea
out east, so we may choose
mountains balanced in an element, or
cold castled ruggedness and thoughts like gales.

To White Moss Wood

A car is coming
and I must wait to cross
as White Moss
Wood must wait for me.

On the other side
the three stone steps are worn
almost away.

Now I'm climbing them
traffic loses its urgency
and all I hear is a treecreeper
displacing quantities of air

as it hops up the trunk.
What happens
in the fifteen minutes before
I look down on a valley?

Local activity.
Wild garlic and fern.
Mud, and the surge
of body heat.

Two Bats

The first I met was a baby,
an accidental landing on the pillow.
Four floors up, the night was hot
and the window wide and receptive as an eye.
Though it hadn't meant to come, its two short flights
cast suspicion on the room, before it joined us, trembling.
In the lamplight it was little more than fur and wing,
no bigger than a thumb; a pulse. Humbled,
it held still as we slid the pint glass under
then raised it slowly to the moon.

The second was sent. Full-grown,
it knew its way around the landscape better than I
who'd thrown the sash down early to inhale the moors –
so it slipped in at dusk unnoticed.
When I hit the switch for the big light
it flung itself back and forth above our heads,
a glove, issuing a challenge over and over.
No instincts rose. Perhaps we were too familiar;
perhaps we already knew that if it settled
we'd be repulsed by black eyes, membranous skin,
bared teeth like a little man's. Instead,
we waited sheepishly on the landing
not looking at much, while someone else
nobler with a tea towel dealt with it.
Afterwards, though we were left to sleep,
something hung on in the dark between us.

Tilt

I'd like to be back in your wheelbarrow,
summer shoes dangling as we charge over
uneven ground towards the finish line –
ignoring the rough rim's burn at the backs
of my knees, the rumble of the loose wheel
vibrating along the length of my spine –
clinging on to the rusted sides,
not knowing if I'm going to tip.

Triple-socked and snow-booted I trudge home.
Walking today demands an effort of mind.
I want to sit down, shut my eyes
and ride the lurch and tilt,
doing whatever I can to maintain
our balance, leaving the rest in your hands.

The Hare

Washed clean at the end
by twenty hours of serious rain,
the remains of a hare are sticking
to the road in front of my house.

With all the dart of it knocked out
there isn't much left to consider:
a stream of southbound traffic has planed
tawny scruff to flat grey.

What mattered were the moments before the sky
let go, which followed its last dash
and the squeal that brought me
to the window

where I saw it laid up on the tarmac
like a hot baby in the act of waking,
coming round to the sense of a mother
somewhere, to justify its reaching,

its mouth closing and opening,
shaping a soundless cry to the morning
and its big black eyes gaping
as though looking for an exit.

Milk

'At one time Johnson apparently owed such a high bill for milk
that his milkman tried to have him arrested.'
Information Panel, Front Hall, Dr Johnson's House, London

When the bailiff knocks he's ready
     in his barricade-bed:
the huge chain slung across the door to keep them out
     and a constant
company in to distract him from his thoughts.

     Upstairs, the scribes
work like seamstresses, piecing together the samples
     he's chosen
from the poets and medicine's contrary wisdom
     (Wiseman: *Milk is the occasion*
of many tumours of divers kinds; Temple: *I concluded, if the gout*
                               continued,

     to confine myself
wholly to the milk diet) to show how words, like things, are
     equivocal. Like

MILK. *n. s.* 1. The liquor with which animals feed their young
    from the breaſt.

Not the liquor most would blame for a debt. But rewind
     to Lichfield, 1709
and see how it cost him from the start: Samuel, the babe who can
                      hardly be
     made to cry,
christened and hastily sent away to a wet nurse *full o' th' milk*
     of human kindness
who infects him as she makes him strong, and leaves him
     boldly scarred;
walking proof of how readily good will can be corrupted.

Cut forward then
to the attic in Gough Square and Lady Macbeth
        rising in his mind,
begging the ministers to *take my milk for gall*.

        Years later, dying
in a borrowed bed, he'll suffer nothing to pass his lips but
        a little, warmed.

The Ways

We fly as the crow does
or the raven, breaking out from his nook in the great tower
to find a new kingdom open before him.

It is clear with this view that sprawl is not the word
for will – our centuries' endeavour,
the making of roads that reach in and out of the city

so that everything leads back to something. Like us
one weekend, scanning thirty-six miles of pavement, canal-side,
verge, forgotten garden in search of your dropped wallet,

weaving eight boroughs into one, from east to west
then home, the route impressed upon your brain
like tyre tracks patterning soft ground.

You twist round corners instinctively. We are drawn uphill by the
promise
of the north-west suburbs relaxing below us. On towpaths
we exchange hellos with strangers, people who know the river

as you know these ways. London's
an original brought to light: the subtle composition
hanging together, entire.

Oxford

1

The sky wasn't thinking of anything in particular.
I saw the woman standing on the bridge –
bare shins
like stalks poking out of the ground
snagged my attention.
The Isis showed her a blank face.

2

The sky's brow was beginning to furrow.
I noticed the woman crossing the high street –
hard feet
dragging and slipping in a man's shoes,
thick coat overloading her bones like a cross.
The city bypassed her as a river moves round an old stone.

3

I had not imagined hearing a woman like that –
her shriek
carving up the afternoon
and lipstick red as hell smeared on her mouth.
The sky knew exactly what to do
and turned its wide back on us both.

German Tinder Box, *c.* 1800

Here's day awaiting itself without realising,
holed up on the mantelpiece in a souvenir tin.
It smells of old conspiring coins:
the morning's tender. Inside it's restless,
flinching in snug dark, dreaming of fire.

Waking is never easy: it happens gradually
with metal, oil, rag, splint; from the patient
clock, clock, clock of flint on steel
a spark is drawn and flown on a paraffin flag
till dawn's incensed, and left to burn.

A box worth more than its weight in gold
to anyone knelt at the cold grate:
to see their own sun born and lifted
out of the heart of a black forest.

Jetsam / Flotsam

Just in

several manuscript variants
of Fortune's tale

each bearing the distinctive
looped cursive
of the sea's editorial.

Titillation for old dogs,
little boys with buckets,
modest treasure hunters.

Grounds for debate
by windswept committees
of sharp-eyed gulls.

*

Floating

between endurance
and the wind's fancy

the ungoverned cargo-states

scrubbed from History's lists
then subjected to the sea's
incessant inventory

the horizon's indifference

and their own
slow disintegration.

Unfathomed
by definition.

25

Ferry Lane

First day of spring. Charm
of goldfinches sounding a
sweet treetop racket.

*

Lone man on a roof
scraping old moss away; grey's
inner red revealed.

*

In the buddleia
behind the recycling bins:
that blackbird, waiting.

*

No smoke without fire.
A smell of coal burning drifts
north off the river.

Linda at Swanfield

From you I learned how portraits give
power to the dead –

the pinpoints of your pupils fixing me
from their fixed centres high on the wall,
regardless of where I stood.

In the daytime your framed presence was a welcome reprieve
from the wallpaper's massive flowers.

In the dark, worried awake, I would try to imagine only
the feel of brushing your long brown hair

but your background was already there, inside my head,
a turquoise so strong and flat it scared me –
as though the man who filled it in knew

how soon only the two dimensions of the painter's
trade would be able to hold you.

Illuminations

Once upon a time – in the twelfth century to be precise – a scribe, hunched
beneath a minuscule high window in a draughty English abbey,
through sheer love of the vellum leaf and his inks (or
perhaps from having been exposed so long to an
ineffectual life among mixed messages)
forgot the established
conventions of
B
(or simply failed
to grasp the notion that some
creatures begin in one way and others
in other ways), so a cat formed in the capital's
hollow, with its muscular tail hanging and its head turned
awkwardly towards the text – as though it could glean an explanation
of the forces that brought it to being and preserved it for close to a millennium.

II

All morning you worked on your initial letter.
At first I watched you – your serious face
magnetised to the most important page
of the new exercise book – the nib
of your tongue tracing each
movement of your hand,
while your other arm
kept your creation
secret in its
elbow's
hollow.
Then
I felt
afraid –
thinking it
possible my
heart would forget
to remain neat, within
the ruled margins of its cage,
and would flail out – an inordinate
scribble of love – precluding at once my
witnessing of all the homeworks yet to come.

The Molecatcher's Warning

Nobody asked or answered questions out there.
Ten miles from the nearest anywhere
the landscape was a disbanded library.

Only the moles remained,
strung on a barbed wire fence,
a dozen antiquated books forced open.

It must've been the north-east wind
or a bandit crow
that picked them over so –

not a scrap hanging on
inside the stretched skins,
their spines disintegrating.

Read in me
they wanted to declare
how it all ends.

But the threads that once
had a hold on their hearts
dangled, loose and crisp.

And their kin
can't read anything
but earth.

Carpe Diem

Surprised by the underside of a snail –
a beige highlight
on an otherwise black window –
I went to the next room for paper and a pen.

I would have sat for hours in the dark
distilling words from it;
studying the plasticine slur,
the way it stuck there
as though on purpose, to rescue
the evening from monotony.

Before I got back
the snail moved on
leaving the window vacant,
a frame to hang a poem on.

On Marriage

Lucky he – little anglerfish
who finds another in vast emptiness
ambivalence impossible
they fuse – symbiotic
so never let go

On land, though
before that bold witness, the sun
how does *she* lure *him*?
what chemicals ride the air between
to hook him on a scented thing?
a self no better than himself
(her blood circulating in her body)
(his blood circulating in his body)
two bodies long distanced from the void
lifted far above deep sea – yet
craving parity – compelled
to attach permanently

a proposal breaches skin
like a bite on the belly

marine snow makes
beautiful confetti

Insomniac

Midnight.
Sky hung like ink in a jar of water.
Moon smooth as a glacier mint on its way to dissolution.

Walking the towpath
cheeks pale
I am dissolving

but not in the way I seek;
not as the mind's fingers reach out
and fuse with the fingers of sleep

to cradle eight hours of dreams; more
as the line between solid and liquid
might be rubbed out,

as path tree grass bench bin everything
blurs. Amid the vagaries
of unsleep

the spirit of the old city is rising like damp,
feeling its blind way back to the fens,
groping at my face and lungs. Here

river has taken to air,
let go of silt,
shrugged off houseboats and swans

to hover over its essence:
to kiss me. When
all I want

is everything to slot into
its proper place:
flat sky, round moon, straight path, dark river.

To lie down still as a woman between new sheets:
eyes closing effortlessly, mind empty
as a jar of water.

Party

The babies don't know how to party.
They just keep on toppling over.
The toddlers don't know how to party.
They're snatching and hitting each other.
The children don't know how to party.
They scream and rebound off each other.
The parents don't know how to party.
They're yawning and hating each other.
My friends used to know how to party.
Today they're all dressed up as mother.

The Met Office Advises Caution

While the river turns up its collar and hurries along,
gulls line up to submit to the weather. One jump

and air possesses them, bodies and wings
helpless as handkerchiefs snatched

from windows of trains intent on the coast.
Each bird is flaunted against the sky,

a warning to any cyclist still clinging on.
Branches lash out; old trees lie down and don't get up.

A wheelie bin crosses the road without looking,
lands flat on its face on the other side, spilling its knowledge.

Split

December drove
a splinter into my thumb,
cleaving skin and nail.
For days I
monitored the digit's
little landscape:
watched the banks
hardening
either side of the red
riverbed
where a stream
glistened and wept.

Cavalier
I skimmed
the dictionary's thin pages,
pressed stamps on anniversary cards,
texted – wincing as I did,
knowing each action
would prolong
the fault.

Healing happened
like a seasonal shift.
Only now I'm
jolted to remember,
speeding round backroads
where last year
rain insinuated itself
into the tiniest
cracks and froze,
splitting the tarmac
then leaving it
potholed.

Pigeons

As your voice pulls away down the line
I picture you: it's warm, and the baby
is in bed, indifferent to daylight,
dreaming of you even while you
confound her imagination.

You are not clearing away the lunch things
or ironing cricket whites for Saturday.
On the carpet the animal alphabet waits
for the sequel to Jellyfish, while Old Macdonald
sits quietly in his tractor under the sofa.

You're standing at the window, transfixed,
as *Columba livia*, estranged from the rocks,
alight in your grid of cabbages.
The motley rabble's nodding insatiably,
haphazardly unpicking your work.

Suddenly everything *pigeon* has flown into
the net of your mind. No matter the glass or garden
separating you from them; you hear them purring
self-congratulatory as cats. A little engine's
encased in each muscular breast.

Not long ago – *thud!* – a renegade interrupted your bed-making,
disturbed the dust on the pane, then fell back
onto the patio and died. One less, you said,
though you waited for it to cool before bagging it up,
double-knotting the handles round its clawed feet.

You're no Darwin. You watch
obsessively; he obsessively *watched
their habits & ways*, and winced

as he laid his favourites down on the table
to administer the fatal dose of ether.

They gave him facts; he repaid them
with handwritten labels
and preservation in a national museum.
But things were different back then.
You have no need for a theory of everything.

On the Proposed Bridge over Ditton Meadow

I do not want to be connected any more
      for my long shadow
the feathered slender grasses and cow-parsley waver in
      to be one among many
caught flickering between the bars of a shadow bridge

I do not want the crooked-faced house
      which nests there, buffered by the broccoli trees like a
                        picture on a jigsaw
or the nettle-paddling herd
      I could almost believe Gilpin had arranged in 1794
eclipsed by the mindset of being on a way somewhere

I do not want to cross the river
      but to be met by the sun
coming down to rest its head upon the water
      while after-dinner blackbirds twirl their elegant proposals
round the fingers of the air

Swing Song

The city is unlatched
    this evening,
    like a back door
flung open to let summer in.

With an irresistible flick
    and arc
    you and I
gather momentum

tipping our heads back,
    swinging horizons
    the wrong way up.
Clouds don't care –

they need only space
    to slide into,
    to streak
bare white against blue

or pose, brazen
    as Miró's abstractions,
    fresh-faced
as graduates.

It's never too late
    to behave like this.
    It's eight
and we're dizzy

but the sun's
    still out
    and nobody's there
to want us back.

Jesus Green

Magpies
potter, content
with the sun's reaction
        to their wings'
blue chemistry.

A figure
        stands, picking
at a ball of foil
in the afternoon's
        fat glare.

        Advancing
        carefully
he stops and bends by each bin
        to prod
the spill of rubbish

        upending a can
at his mouth
                awaiting the trickle

        then shaking a packet
to empty
its corner of crisps.

Fearlessness of wasps
is a state of mind
        he has mastered.

Picnickers dotted around
        can't help
but watch him scrutinise
the scrap of silver:

man
               mid-forties
in a smart black jacket
         in June
absorbing a heatwave.

Ickworth

An estate
is too far.
Panoramic,
neat, historical,
unpeopled.

A curve of sandstone,
an arc of lavender,
the sense of green
spreading below the feet:
this scale of things
we might manage.

But look at that bee,
focused on the job
of applying and re-
applying its perfect body
to the mauve universe.

The longer we watch
the more there are
and lavender has black
spots and is moving in
plain sight, though we
hadn't noticed before.

Visitor

I find myself standing in the garden
among familiars: pink and yellow roses;
an anniversary birdbath now wrapped in moss;
the stone-grey football that soaks up water
and wheezes like an old man. On the ridged path
loose soil shifts between my toes.

I reach over the back fence, unbolt the gate,
sidestep the fat blackcurrant bush
and weave through avenues of runner beans.
In the heat of the greenhouse, time breathes
slowly, the air heavy as tomatoes;
the same air that hung about your hands.

I make an inventory: cracked flowerpots;
radio components awaiting reincarnation;
spilt seeds still clinging to dreams of geraniums.
I close the door. The sun stays inside, dozing.
In the shade of the laburnum your collection of rain
is brimming again. I deliver it. It keeps returning.

Flesh & Bone

Two freaks displayed in the Hunterian Museum

DANIEL LAMBERT (1770–1809)

Up to his neck in flesh, the famous fat man of Georgian England
deposits himself on a double chair forever. Why we do not know,
nor at what or whom he gazes roundly, and without acuity, as
though such bulk necessitated sluggishness of perception also.

What's saved him, from the eighteenth century's gloom and his
own beige prison, is that coat – flowing, bright as blood, parted
like a mouth about to let us in on a big secret: something about
proportion, without which history looks like a too-recent joke.

CHARLES BYRNE (1761–1783)

These long femurs
he bequeathed
to the sea,
or as good as did
– shelled out
sacks of coins
in exchange
for promises
of protection
after death. Rather
be nibbled gently,
smoothed to extinction,
than subjected
to the surgeon's
excoriating fingers,
exacting measures
and, God
forbid, that
boiling pot.

Betrayed
he stands
emptied
of growing pains,
empty of all
loyalties
to Ireland
and its
High Kings,
his phoney lineage.
The burden
of self-supporting
relieved
by a toolkit
of wires and pins.
No time
without flesh.
Old air in
a glass case.

And to look at,
such an
ordinary skull,
resisting expansion
in the usual
ways; hardly
a phrenologist's
dream. But
engraved
on the inside
with a fighting story,
his hormones'
wild urge
to grow and
grow and pay
no heed
to the fixed
boundary
of his frame.

Cynosure

When the thin chain snapped
a diamond heart broke free,

hit the floor with a plop
too loud for its small mass

and a single, flat bounce:
slow motion

during which I supposed
three years close to my chest

had imparted to it
a heaviness it couldn't bear.

Up it stared from the carpet,
a bright lidless eye

glinting in its silver socket.
Carbon to the core

I stared back hard.

When you have a baby

please don't cease
to enquire after anyone else

or ask me a question
as though to suggest you cared for the answer
then three words in cut it off
to provide a commentary on your child's completely
unextraordinary observable behaviour

or invite me to be godmother
knowing full well I could never
renounce an acquaintance I've met only
once, in a poem, so am not equipped to judge

but most importantly

please don't call it
Ezra
Emmeline
Sylvia
Jacob
Cecily
Freda
Meredith
Hope
Isaac
Lavender
Erin
Arthur
Reuben
Azalea
Polly
Heidi
Lettice
Melody
Nathaniel
or May

just in case just in case just in case just in case

Focal Periosteal Reaction Seen in Distal Fibula

Like a comet
trailing flame across a hitherto unsensational sky
this burning in my bone
has lit up the usual absence of pain.

Distances have changed:
each skip from bedroom to kitchen to study
an expedition; the library shifted
further from the bike shed; the supermarket's aisles stretching
on and on,
unmanageable alone.

I gather the laces in my hand
and swing the running shoes out of sight,
precious cushion soles treading air.

Hunger is the only safe activity.
I vow to get good at it.

After rain

here's mist
slung like a belt on the evening's waist

here's nettle and thistle's
uprisings, suppressed

there's the herd,
huddled, waiting for blindness to lift

here's a cloudmass
stretching to the far-off edge

there's the city,
a mirage crowned with red

here's a fisherman
in silhouette

the flicker of a pipistrelle
overhead

plink
of surface tension punctured by a fish

Lodge Farm

Sixteen years will have shifted since the night we stood
with the moon and an unhitched wagon of pumpkins in the yard,
coat sleeves pushed up over our elbows, breath like spirits.
Our big knives twisted and sliced, cleaved flesh to make bone,
hollowed eyes. We scooped mulch out in palmfuls and set aglow
a line of gormless faces, each one insensible of its loss.

Now it's September and we're stooped in rows in the orchard,
the last of the low sun on our shoulders, cheeks russetted,
tossing windfalls into buckets. Later we'll take turns at the table:
halve, crush and shovel the fruit into your grandfather's wooden box,
press down the lid, borrow a man to turn the crank; watch as the liquid
pools in the gulley, spills over and is funnelled into fat glass bottles.

We'll collect a cupboardful and wait; look forward; light a bonfire,
stand about and talk until we're stood in the dark, wondering
when the sun went down. Then some philosopher ablaze on last year's
cider will look up and say *that's how it goes* – we remember the sun
and the dark, not the day growing old. It's overlooked, what happens
in the middle. Like the browning of an apple once it's bitten.

Dove Cottage

In bed
they shift

hearing the lock snap,
the click as she lifts the latch,

but keep their eyes shut.
Marriage must accommodate,

for which of them
would want to brave the pre-dawn

cold, to lay the fires? Their work
starts later:

open dealings with the lakes and fells;
tending to the burden of an attic mind.

Clock cuckoos.
By noon

bright flames worry sweat
from the poet's high forehead.

While he muses
a woman's hand hovers

like a writer's,
itching to distil

each drop of his labour
into verse.

Moments crackle;
her pen scratches the paper.

Confession

I live alone and talk to the spiders.

Reader, do not believe this is a character
poem; this is your poet speaking.

In a modern house a spider is a jagged
thing – atavistic
disturber of magnolian serenity.

Here
where the walls have texture
and decorate themselves at night with their own shadows
and the windows are open
even when they're shut
a spider
       curled up in a corner
             or hanging softly
exudes an aura of benevolence.

As all my spiders look the same
       a neat brown **8**
the impression I've got is of a single
guardian spider mirroring my movements,
unassuming, but omniscient.

To my guardian over the shower I sing
scales and renderings of English folk ballads.

To my guardian beside the desk I enumerate
the annoyances and the benefits
of freelance editing assignments.

To my guardian above the bed I whisper
words of gravity-defying encouragement,
hoping its bird's-eye view will outlast sleep
> and it won't
> lower itself
> to my level
> or the level
> of the half-
> full glass
> I'll reach
> for in the
> gloom.

But to the lapsed guardian
who dashes from behind the fruit bowl across the white worktop
I cry *no!* and with a deftness that surprises

me, in one seamless motion
grab a party invitation and scoop up the shock
and shake it out into the dark.

Then I feel so very self-consciously
human, under the kitchen light with my instinct
and lonely efficiency, and don't say anything.

Turning

Now it's autumn
and another year in which I could leave you
is a slowly sinking ship.

The air has developed edges
and I am preparing to let myself lie
in a curtained apartment,

safe in the knowledge that strangers
have ceased to gather and laugh
in the lane below

and the brazen meadow no longer
presumes to press its face to the window
like an inquisitor.

Soon even the river will evince a thicker skin,
my breath each morning will flower white,
and all of summer's schemes will fly like cuckoos.

The leaves are turning and the trees
are shaking them off. Bonfire smoke
between us like a promise lingers.

Spiritus Mundi Reloaded

When I asked you in an email what the new songs you were writing were about, replies came fast: *Co-codamol. Turkmenistan. Teapot potteries. Toronto boshes. The number 54.8.*

Echolaliac! Although the time you waste entertaining (let alone typing) such phrases is time not spent fine-tuning original thoughts – and while in your presence answers of this kind elicit my extreme irritation – silent on the screen they struck me as auspicious. And having just finished a stint with William James and been privy to his notion of a universal consciousness, I went online to search for meaning in your choice of 54.8.

(You'll claim you plucked it from the air, but nothing is random – the world's a Rubik's Cube the mind seizes in its labourer's grip and manipulates till the colours come round to sense.) Now I am aware

that in the Samyutta Nikaya of the *Tipitaka* the Buddha reminds us to practise the basic principle, mindfulness of breathing: so that to breathe in steadies the mind; to breathe out steadies the mind; to breathe in releases the mind; to breathe out releases the mind; so the mind, through complete control, is let go. So the mind flows

into mind. Could this explain why 54.8 is the latitude of your favourite city – another fact I discerned from the god-shaped cloud, concatenator of disparate knowns, analogue of the Great One Mind, with which we don't have to commune for long before we can apprehend each of the Buddha's discourses, or the satellites' dispassionate measure of a world?

Generally I regret the substitution of hyperlinks for attention, of superficial connections for the effort of thought. Today I let myself go, clicking and tapping on instinct, like a bird breaking into a golf ball, and extracted what I hadn't known I sought – a kernel of something – substance, in the end, for a kind of poem.

Emperor Penguin

The Polar Museum, Cambridge

This afterlife
is inaccurate: everything here is dry.

I try to make
a true impression, but the chick

I've been given
refuses to play the part, persists with its leaning

as if it could
imagine anything beyond our destiny.

Before I was seized
my throat was an open channel,

my beak
a conduit for the sea. It is not shame

that forces
my head to hang: it is the inured act

I've grown too stiff
to shake off. Chick, even like this

you look hungry.
There is no escape. Turn in and face up.

Aldeburgh Beach

Sea coming
brown Sea falling over itself like an itchy bear
Sea blustering, hands in the air
gesturing *me me*
Sea slanting rhythmically north
but I'm here
Sea sounding off
always Sea yielding
froth

Night Owl

Your call comes clambering over the dark
to find me: electronic, futuristic.
The valley shoulders the sound, shudders.

I run through the night, our lives run
parallel, unbridged except by this metallic
whip, this whirring from your skull, this
echo caught in my temporal lobe.

What do you see? I can't make out
my feet, let alone the hollow you're in,
soliciting, at an orbit's edge.

Current (I) = charge (Q) ÷ time (t)

The LED, control switch, wires, crocodile clips, battery:
that was physics; an anxiety. Now we are connected

long-distance, and I am anxious to touch your arm, my fingers
relaying the charge, to complete the circuit: this is chemistry.

Brontë

Plait my hair
plait it and wind it to form
a beguiling mathematical band with no visible end.

Make my face bare
make it mirror plain truth
never graced with the lie of a word like prettiness.

Strip me down
how you'd strip down a dolly
whose clothes must be freed of the familiar scent

and re-dress me:
petticoat, undershirt, overskirt,
pinafore, thick woollen stockings and cloak.

Boots I must lace
for boots must be sure as the day
ten miles each day, to collect or deliver a letter

or despair
fly west and later retread
arriving weak and pale as a morning moon.

Take me in
I won't beg or instruct
chastened by the sky's running always down off the hills

bound homeward
in love with and afraid of fire
learning to forget my given name.

Deep Six

now you've gone down
and retrieval isn't possible

now there's no chance of you
washing up on any shore

I find I can cast off
at night

in a boat I do not own
and row

straight into the middle of the lake
(too deep for police divers to check)

and there when everything is still
take from my pocket a stone

and hold it over the side
and let it go

how easy it is

opening my hand above the water
seeing your white face goggle

(and the cold)
(and the pressure)

as the glow of your outstretched fingers recedes
I pull my head through the noose

of my sweater
and breathe

Antarctica

Heaven   is a sweet dream   Tinned peaches and syrup   sweeter

Awake   listening   in the dark   frenzy of canvas   wind   slapping

like so many frozen hands   Body   a quaker   Muscles crying

sugar   Tired   as a dog   but colder   *Colder*

Language   is a beggar   Hope   another

Land of the South   pure   and Beauty   enough   to transfix or unfix

to turn a man's eyes blue   and Hope   they say   is a blue-eyed look

God   sender of daylight   scatterer of the terrors of the dark   planter

of strenuous prayers in the heart   Heart   keeper of the flesh   Heartbeat

a song   a step   a prayer   *Heave*

what a man must do   for God   for glory   for mercy

Bird like a snowflake like God   glittering   in a blue sky   lucent as an angel's wing

Gift   given freely   with both hands   This Earth   is a good place

to live in   Die   as everything must   Numb   as a mass

of ice   frozen reindeer bag   coffin   crevasse   A good warm sleep

a wish   *Great God!*   *this is an awful place*

Give take   Take   give   Keep temper   don't speak   God is

grace   Returning   a certain numbed pleasure   biscuit   talk

write   rest   *sleep*   Comfort   of the Almighty's making

Peace   in the satisfaction of faith   *drifting*   eyes open

All   that the Lord has given   taken away   Blessed

Footnote

Tiny red leaf
I keep

long after
the sprig of oak

I picked
and wore in my hair

(which made a woman
in the café speak to me)

has yellowed, cracked
and gone to the bin:

memento
of your sharper eye;

gleaned
from deep drifts of brown

here on my shelf
means what it means.

Advent

You call, and I imagine you entirely
as though I were the swirl of smoke,
the updraught and enigma
held warm in your mouth.

I hold my breath, wait to be released,
to mix with the safe undarkness
of your cul-de-sac.

To be there; to hang for a second or more
in a Christmas night's incurious air,
clear of hope and intent, in a place which
as yet expects nothing of me: yes,

yes to the whole idea. And the process,
if it's to be anything like this;
unwinding, beginning at your lips.

Christmas Day

Home, yes
unmarried, yes
     but how I go

zip up my coat
show my back to the gaudy telly
     and step out

How the cold boxes my ears

Last hour of light
I follow the fade uphill
     (big strides, incremental dark)

to the bench gone fuzzy with old rain
and sit, letting it
     all sink in

Landlocked valley
the grey-blue clouds are my estuary
     my far-off hills

gold ribbon song of
seen and hiding blackbirds
     my company

and all the trees
like disciples, arms thrown up
     in love

or surrender, or
whatever they hold themselves
     open for

Long Jump

I don't have to take a run-up any more.
I haven't measured out my approach in advance
in pigeon steps. I didn't spend Tuesday afternoon
tiptoeing on imaginary eggshells
or Thursday slouching backwards down the lane
loosening each muscle's hold on its bone.

To start up from zero and gather speed
and feel myself opening out like a hairpin,
crescendo right up to the bam of the board,
toes pushing, arch lifting, knee driving, and fly –
and hang before the silent drop,
moving through stillness, arms outstretched,

is rare now. I don't need to brush myself off
and walk away as though I don't care for the result.
But I sometimes jog down Wilberforce Road to the track,
over which a grey sky's spread; where crows
saunter by stray hockey balls, and the wind
sweeps across unimpeded from Siberia.

Notes

LETTER FROM CHINA: The phrases 'a daughter is like spilled water' and 'bare branches' are proverbial in China, as cited by Steven Pinker in *The Better Angels of Our Nature* (London: Penguin, 2012, p. 508 and pp. 830–31).

GERMAN TINDER BOX, c. 1800: William and Dorothy Wordsworth brought a tinder box back from their travels in the Black Forest in 1799; until very recently it sat on the kitchen mantelpiece in Dove Cottage, the house in Grasmere where they lived with Mary Wordsworth and others between 1799 and 1808.

ILLUMINATIONS: Part I was prompted by a detail in a twelfth-century psalter held in St John's College Library, Cambridge (MS K. 30, f. 104v).

ON MARRIAGE: This poem paraphrases a section of David Attenborough's commentary from episode two of *The Blue Planet* (BBC, 2005).

ON THE PROPOSED BRIDGE OVER DITTON MEADOW: William Gilpin (1724–1804) was the author of a series of books on picturesque beauty, based on his observations of the British countryside and illustrated with his sketches.

DEEP SIX: The title is a nautical expression indicating a water depth of six fathoms (36 ft), traditionally thought to be the minimum depth required for a sea burial.

ANTARCTICA: Some of the words in this poem are taken from the accounts of the 1910–1913 British Antarctic Expedition (Terra Nova) and Apsley Cherry-Garrard's 1922 retrospective *The Worst Journey in the World*.

Acknowledgements

Acknowledgements are due to the editors of the following publications, in which versions of some of these poems previously appeared: *Angle*, *Crabbe Poetry Prize Anthology* (Suffolk Poetry Society), *Cycle Lifestyle*, *Einstein & the Art of Mindful Cycling* (Leaping Hare Press, 2012), *The Fenland Reed*, *Die Gazette*, *Magma*, *Mslexia*, *New Poetries VI: An Anthology* (Carcanet, 2015), *The North* and *PN Review*. 'Emperor Penguin' and 'Antarctica' were commissioned by The Polar Museum, Cambridge as part of The Polar Muse project (2014).

For their inspiration, generous encouragement and invaluable criticisms, I am indebted to Ben Irvine, Jacob Polley, Sarah Hall, Penny Boxall, Claudine Toutoungi, Adam Crothers, James Richards and Michael Schmidt.